FOR EACH OTHER

Historic Ethnic Fraternal Organizations in the Old Cities

Janet Anderson

Author: Janet Gerilyn Anderson PhD
Publisher: Gaelic League Cultural Consortium
Cover: Jennifer Valente
Printed in the United States

Cover photos (credits): front left: Bohemian National Hall in Cleveland (author); front center: Gaelic League of Detroit hearth (author); front right: Adam Mickiewicz Library and Dramatic Circle (forgottenbuffalo.com); rear top: Detroit Boat Club 1902 headquarters (Detroit Publishing Company); rear bottom: Milwaukee Turnverein, late 19th century (public domain).

Photo credits: care was taken to establish rights and seek permissions in the use of photos not in the public domain; care was taken to source photos in the public domain.

Copyright 2020

TABLE OF CONTENTS

PREFACE

1. **WHY FRATERNAL ORGANIZATIONS? WHY ETHNIC CLUBS?** 1
   Pouring into Cities and Seeking Their Own Clubs 6
   Tables: Detroit's ethnic populations (1880-1900); Irish immigrants (1820-2004) 8
   Emergence of Ethnic Clubs 9
   The Interesting Case of Irish Organizations in America 12
   Do Ethnic Clubs Unite or Divide? 26

2. **FRATERNAL ETHNIC CLUBS TODAY** 27
   Baltimore's Arch Social Club 28
   Buffalo's Adam Mickiewicz Library and Dramatic Circle 30
   Cleveland's Bohemian National Hall 31
   Gaelic League Irish American Club of Detroit 33
   Milwaukee, Philadelphia and Cleveland Turner Societies 34
   Philadelphia's Palizzi Social Club 37
   Pittsburgh's Teutonia Mannerchor 39
   Pittsburgh's John Kollar Literary and Library Society 41
   San Francisco's The Polish Club Inc 42
   San Francisco Italian Athletic Club 44

3. **FRATERNAL ORGANIZATIONS OPERATING HISTORIC CLUBHOUSES IN DETROIT TODAY** 47
    A Powerful Legacy Still Evident in Detroit's Building Stock 49
    Detroit Boat Club Crew 52
    Detroit Yacht Club 54
    Detroit Club 56
    Detroit Athletic Club 58
    Yondotega Club 59
    Detroit Golf Club 61
    Indian Village Tennis Club 63
    Bayview Yacht Club 65
    Gaelic League Irish American Club of Detroit 67
    Kappa Alpha Psi Fraternity, Inc – Historic Detroit Alumni Chapter 69
    Omega Psi Phi Fraternity – Nu Omega Chapter 69
    Detroit Maltese-American Benevolent Society 71

POSTSCRIPT: HOW FRATERNAL CLUBS ARE ASSURING THEIR VITALITY 72
    Strategic Planning and Marketing of History 72
    Creating Trusts and Charitable 501c.3 Conservancies 73
    Forming Alliances and Consortia 73

TO READ MORE ABOUT IT 74

Dedication:

To people who believe in each other, understand where they came from, and commit to making their communities better. Nothing else ever mattered in America.

PREFACE

Clubhouse-based fraternal organizations are enjoying a bit of a renaissance in the old cities, in no small part due to reinvestment in the cities themselves. In Detroit, the number of historic social clubs that are thriving, or in the process of refurbishment, includes:

- Detroit Boat Club (originally formed 1839)
- Detroit Yacht Club (originally formed 1868)
- Detroit Club (originally formed 1882, reopened 2018)
- Detroit Athletic Club (originally formed 1887)
- Yondotega Club (1891)
- Detroit Golf Club (1899)
- Bayview Yacht Club (1915)

The Gaelic League of Detroit joins the list of organizations building on their long, impressive traditions. Formed in 1920 to keep alive culture endangered in the Irish homeland fighting to escape centuries of colonization, the organization has been a fixture with a dynamic agenda of year-round activities for members and the community. The clubhouse is in the heart of

Corktown's main street, Michigan Avenue, in Detroit's old Irish and oldest existing neighborhood where the club intends to remain for a second century.

Cities are littered with evidence of the time when clubs were everywhere. The clubs focused not on profits but on people – on "fraternal" activities, if member-based; or on charitable activities if public-facing. Most fraternal clubs went the way of history, as populations spread out and neighborhood-based living became an exception; some evolved from fraternal in nature, to commercial or to charitable purposes. Many historic clubhouse buildings remain. This book celebrates the survivors: the fraternal clubs still operating their historic clubhouses in Detroit, and the fraternal ethnic clubs still in their clubhouses in big cities where most immigrants arrived. The book highlights the evolution of Irish ethnic clubs as an example of this long journey.

The Gaelic League of Detroit celebrates its 100th anniversary and the great traditions of fraternal clubs and of historic urban places. Reinvestment in Detroit has spurred a new era in club life, but the act of gathering itself is the formula for these clubs' successes. People like to affiliate, and clubs add to the mix that is keeping cities vital for a new generation.

WHY FRATERNAL ORGANIZATIONS? WHY ETHNIC CLUBS?

Fraternal organizations – also known as "mutual aid societies" or "social clubs" – were a special counterweight to unbridled commercial enterprise in 19th century America. They were intense, splashy, innovative, mysterious and elegantly simple beings. They built community and bridged people's needs. These organizations were places of connection and belonging, initially organizing skilled artisans, and then offering real opportunities for organized recreation.

Before industrialization ushered in big business, mysterious secret societies such as Freemasons and Knights Templar showed eccentric flashes but lived mostly behind secret passwords. The Independent Order of the Oddfellows, with its colorful uniform regalia, was probably Detroit's most prominent secret society before the Civil War.

The bigger that American businesses became, fraternal clubs multiplied in number and type, in membership, and ultimately, in impact. More people had leisure time, and business clubs, university clubs and athletic clubs emerged for them in every city.

The Union Club in New York (1836) and the Detroit Boat Club (1839) are among the nation's earliest fraternal organizations still in existence. The Union Club formed to facilitate business. The Detroit Boat Club formed out of interest in rowing as athletics gained importance. Both built edifices that became hubs of their organizations and landmarks.

Figure 1 - The Chicago Club is representative of the business organizations that formed downtown in every City in this period. SOURCE: Detroit Publishing Company, 1905.

Growth of these societies was so exponential that a landmark study of fraternal organizations was prepared in 1902 (Meyer). The study found:

- From 1880-1890: the number of lodges in metro centers grew from 10 to 158
- From 1893-1900: U.S. membership grew from 3.7 million to 5.3 million. 50 secret societies – fraternities and Grand Army of the Republic veterans – added millions.
- Of 568 fraternal societies existing in 1901, only 202 had been formed before 1890
- In 1900, the national federation of the societies held $4 billion in insurance policies on which was paid out $38 million in benefits.

The practice of "Mutual Aid" originated with the Ancient Order of The United Workmen in Meadville, Pennsylvania (1868) who collected members' payments into a fund for death and disability support. It was so popular that local lodges and Elks clubs formed and fraternal organizations in 1900 paid $38 million to widows, children and disabled workers. With no pensions and health benefits, these organizations became prominent. When a national income tax was instituted in 1913, fraternal organizations were exempted in recognition of all they did for members.

By 1916, the National Tourist Board called Detroit a top convention destination, many of which were gatherings of fraternal clubs (Loomis, 2015). Detroit set a goal of becoming a headquarters city for the organizations.

Figure 2 – LEFT: December 29, 1907, ProQuest Historical Newspapers: Detroit Free Press p.12.
RIGHT: Sep 4, 1907; ProQuest Historical Newspapers: Detroit Free Press p.9.

Figure 3 – High profile of fraternal clubs in Detroit. LEFT: Apr 23, 1919; ProQuest Historical Newspapers: Detroit Free Press p.17. RIGHT: Nov 2, 1917. ProQuest Historical Newspapers, Detroit Free Press, p.3.

Stereoscopic views, mid-19th century technology for three-dimensional images, were compiled for fraternal organizations in Boston. The Masonic Temple, Odd Fellows Hall and other clubs were documented for tourists in the pairs of slightly offset images. Simultaneous right and left eye looks gave depth to the images, bringing the buildings to life.

Figure 4 - Odd Fellows' Hall, Boston (1875). SOURCE: Miriam and Ira D. Wallach Division of Art, Prints and Photographs: Photography Collection. Courtesy of The New York Public Library. www.nypl.org.

POURING INTO CITIES AND SEEKING THEIR OWN CLUBS.

By mid-19th century, people from all over the world were pouring into America's urban centers. Immigrants had been pushed out of their homelands by hunger, like the 1840s famine Irish or peasant Poles in the 1870s. Or, they were pushed out by political upheaval, like the Czech "48'ers" escaping Austrian oppression or early 19th century Germans.

The story of ethnic fraternal organizations starts with industrialization. 19th century economic growth only happened with large numbers of people. The undeveloped countryside and people largely from Europe flooded into the Great Cities: the coastal colonies of Boston, New York, Philadelphia, Baltimore and San Francisco; the waterways of St Louis, Cincinnati, and Chicago; and industrial centers Buffalo, Pittsburgh, Cleveland, Milwaukee, and Detroit.

Few arrived with anything other than the language and customs of home. They arrived in the bottom of steamers that cost every cent and barely offered space for a trunk. The largest ethnic groups moving here were Poles, Italians, German, and Irish, but every corner of Europe was part of this movement.

They built roads, bridges and other systems, creating opportunities that pulled in other immigrants. Miles and miles of building expanded the shapes of towns, until a quilt of neighborhoods new and old was stitched together. These neighborhoods concentrated ethnic groups, and they formed businesses, churches, newspapers, and other organizations that facilitated exchange of ideas and resources. It was natural for the growing numbers of foreign-born to build their fraternal organizations as well, focused on their social needs and interests, in neighborhoods where they lived.

Detroit's Ethnic Populations in Ethnic Neighborhoods 1880-1900		
ethnicity	% Clustered 1880	% Clustered 1900
American	37.61	51.5
Canadian	17.47	na
English Canadian	Na	20.08
French Canadian	Na	30.76
British	13.73	12.39
Irish	40.74	40.56
German	52.43	58.62
Polish	70.49	82.1
Russian	Na	57.5

4.7 Million Irish Immigrants to America (1820–2004)			
Period	Number of immigrants	Period	Number of immigrants
1820–1830	54,338	1911–1920	146,181
1831–1840	207,381	1921–1930	211,234
1841–1850	780,719	1931–1940	10,973
1851–1860	914,119	1941–1950	19,789
1861–1870	435,778	1951–1960	48,362
1871–1880	436,871	1961–1970	32,996
1881–1890	655,482	1971–1980	11,940
1891–1900	388,416	1981–1990	31,969
1901–1910	399,065	1991–2004	62,447

Figure 5 - LEFT: Olivier Zunz, "Detroit's Ethnic Neighborhoods at the end of the Nineteenth Century," University of Michigan. August 1977 (rev. Feb 1978). Table 6 (p.53). RIGHT: U.S. Bureau of Census, Decennial Census of Population.

America would expand from sea to shining sea with torches lit, or protected, by organizations. Fraternal organizations were an important ingredient; charitable organizations were another. B'Nai B'Rith, translated as "Children of the Covenant," formed in New York City in 1843 to provide social reform and uplift, and opened Covenant House (1851), the first Jewish fraternal center in America, and a Jewish Public Library and Orphanage. New York's University Settlement (1886) and Jane Addams' Hull House in Chicago (1889) bridged the gaps of urban poor who couldn't find housing, education, medical care or employment.

Charitable, welfare-oriented organizations brought people together much as fraternal clubs did. Unlike ethnic fraternal clubs, they were neither administered by, nor fluent in the cultural traditions of, the immigrants they served. The social reform movement probably peaked when the Polish National Alliance Chicago branch created the Polish Welfare Association (PWA, 1922) to minister to new Polish immigrants. The organization was briefly operated by the Chicago Archdiocese and in 1976 became a not-for-profit organization (under section 501.c.3 of the IRS Tax Code) with the name "Polish American Association" to reflect a decreasing emphasis on new immigrants, who were decreasing in number.

These social welfare agencies provided some measure of brotherhood around their service but were not membership-based like the fraternal clubs: operated by and for the people having the specific common interest.

EMERGENCE OF ETHNIC CLUBS.

Ethnic clubs, such as Teutonia Mannerchor of Pittsburgh (1854), brought fraternal organizations from the waterfronts and city centers, to the neighborhoods. With ethnic groups clustered together out of convenience and necessity, it was logical to build clubhouses where they lived, and Teutonia Mannerchor built in the Deutschtown section of Pittsburgh's North Shore, where German immigrants concentrated.

Ethnic clubs served several purposes:
- Advocating for reforms to deal with challenges faced by immigrants
- Devising tools for mutual aid, like insurance, to help members adjust in a new world
- Offering leads on jobs or support for new businesses
- Providing emotional support through socializing such as sharing cultural traditions

Clubs provided wholesome activities that kept men out of taverns and boys out of the rough city streets. Many a tavern eagerly separated men from earnings needed to support their families, and many a boy was led into harm's way as a result. The clubs taught men English and connected them to work, housing or sales opportunities.

Many of the organizations were for men only in a time where traditional gender roles were the norm. They were nonpolitical and not related to a religious sect. They weren't always run according to management standards but gave people opportunities to show their talents and hone new skills as leaders. On occasion, this could lead to financial difficulties, or fraud. People wanted to gather, and to lay roots for future generations, and they became part of the infrastructure that attracted even more immigrants.

Many groups started in church spaces or in homes, like Buffalo's Adam Mickiewicz Library and Dramatic Circle, which went from the home of a prominent journalist, to a room in St Stanislaus, the largest church in Buffalo's Polonia. Cleveland's Hungarian Benevolent Aid Society (now the Heights Benevolent and Social Union) operated from a number of sites for 100 years. The German Turnvereins, or "Turners," continually added recreational facilities sufficient to providing the athletic opportunities at the core of their mission.

Some groups had difficulty securing their own clubhouses. The Gaelic League of Detroit started a Building Fund in the 1920s which was depleted by aid to members during the Great Depression in America's hardest hit big city. African-Americans trickled into cities from the post-reconstruction south, and they too formed institutions, mostly focused on political rights or economic opportunities reflecting their legal status. Their newspapers, civil rights groups, and entertainment clubs have left a significant legacy. Having arrived to America in bondage, and arrived to cities as second-class citizens under the law, African-Americans had few resources to buy buildings. Journalist and NAACP co-founder Ida B. Wells' clubs in Chicago, site of the largest Black migration, never established permanent clubhouses.

Today, fraternal organizations hold tax exemption under section c.7 of the Federal Tax Code Chapter 501, recognizing that they convey collective benefit to their members. They are thus well-known as "501.c.7" organizations. Section c.3 of the same code is the best known of these exemptions; "501.c.3" organizations exist to service a public purpose and have proliferated in part due to their appeal to philanthropic funders.

THE INTERESTING CASE OF IRISH ORGANIZATIONS IN AMERICA.

Irish Americans have a rich history organizing ethnic societies. The early ones aligned with ancestral experiences, then, for benevolent, or charitable or purposes related to Irish Americans in need. Some clubs were formed for fraternization. The fraternal organizations focused on building clubhouses. Today, this dynamic history has led to a new breed of cultural center combining the same purposes with educational and artistic interpretative materials.

Ancient Order of Hibernians.

The Ancient Order of Hibernians (AOH) is one of the oldest of Irish charitable organizations in America. The AOH was founded at New York's St. James Church in 1836 to protect Irish Catholic immigrants and their churches from Nativist attacks, and as such, is a continuation of Ireland's secret societies under English domination. The influx of immigrants fleeing Ireland's famine prompted many Irish societies, much as early societies in occupied Ireland protected Catholics, and the clergy who risked death to keep Catholicism alive under Penal Laws. As societies formed, the need to incorporate in one name became evident and in 1851, New York State registered the Ancient Order of Hibernians.

Though its motto is "Friendship, Unity, and Christian Charity," the early AOH in America remained defensive and secret, and little is known of specific activities. Membership was well-guarded and restricted to Irish-born, until opened to Irish Americans so that American-born sons of immigrants could join, and to grow loyalty to America.

The AOH was not just in big cities. It tracked the Lewis and Clark Trail (St Anne's in Great Falls, MT), the Cherokee trail (Sacred Heart in Pueblo, CO) and alongside the Central Pacific Railroad from Ogden, UT (St. Joseph's) to Sacramento, CA (Old Cathedral). Hibernians shared meeting halls with other fraternal societies. By the mid-1800s, the AOH had become American; yet, it always acknowledged roots in those societies organized to defend Gaelic values and heritage. Today, AOH supports charity, education, the church, and patriotism.

Clan-na-Gael.

The revolutionary Clan-na-Gael organization was founded in New York City, in 1867. The word Fenian came to be used for groups that shared the Clan-na-Gael's goal of an independent Ireland, even if by force. Several distinct secret organizations included the Fenians, founded in New York in 1858 and the Irish Republican Brotherhood, founded in Dublin in 1858.

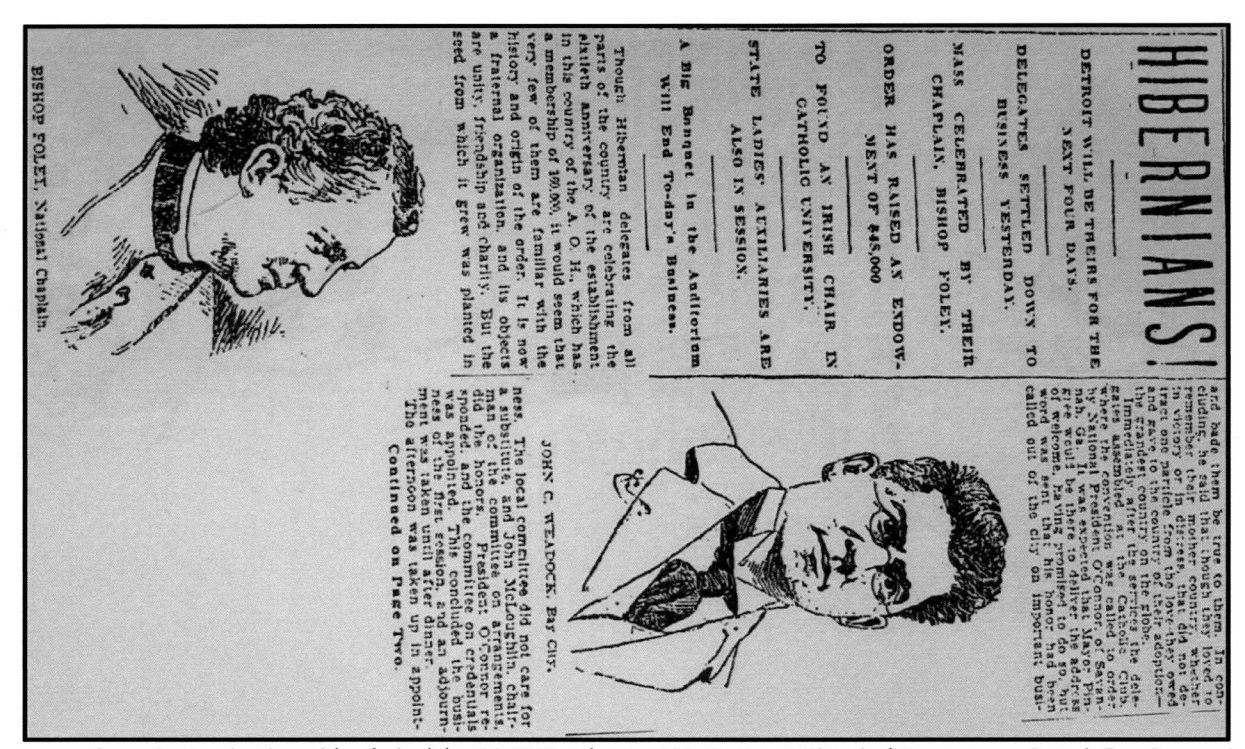

Figure 6 – Fascination with ethnic clubs. SOURCE: July 15, 1896; ProQuest Historical Newspapers, Detroit Free Press p.1.

In Cleveland, the Westside Irish American Club (WSIA) was formed at the same time as Cleveland's Terence MacSwiney Club, a Clan-na-Gael organization that shared many members. The WSIA was intentionally not focused on politics and concentrated on celebrating Irish cultural traditions. Some early members of Detroit's Gaelic League were Clan-na-Gael, which caused some conflict among club members.

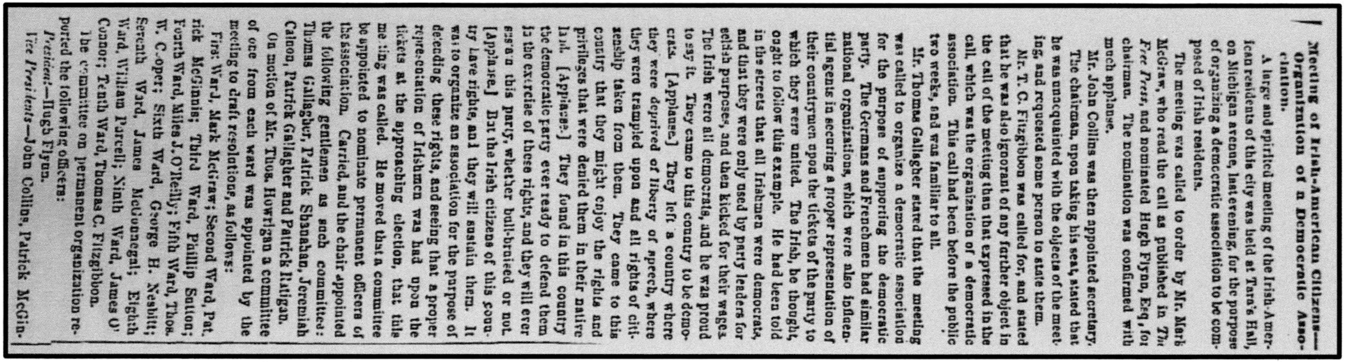

Meeting of Irish-American Citizens—Organization of a Democratic Association.

A large and spirited meeting of the Irish-American residents of this city was held at Tara's Hall, on Michigan avenue, last evening, for the purpose of organizing a democratic association to be composed of Irish residents.

The meeting was called to order by Mr. Mark McGraw, who read the call as published in *The Free Press*, and nominated Hugh Flynn, Esq., for chairman. The nomination was confirmed with much applause.

Mr. John Collins was then appointed secretary.

The chairman, upon taking his seat, stated that he was unacquainted with the objects of the meeting, and requested some person to state them.

Mr. T. C. Fitzgibbon was called for, and stated that he was also ignorant of any farther object in the call of the meeting than that expressed in the call, which was the organization of a democratic association. This call had been before the public two weeks, and was familiar to all.

Mr. Thomas Gallagher stated that the meeting was called to organize a democratic association for the purpose of supporting the democratic party. The Germans and Frenchmen had similar national organizations, which were also influential agents in securing a proper representation of their countrymen upon the tickets of the party to which they were united. The Irish, he thought, ought to follow this example. He had been told in the streets that all Irishmen were democrats, and that they were only used by party leaders for selfish purposes, and then kicked for their wages. The Irish were all democrats, and he was proud to say it. They came to this country to be democrats. [Applause.] They left a country where they were deprived of liberty of speech, where they were trampled upon and all rights of citizenship taken from them. They came to this country that they might enjoy the rights and privileges that were denied them in their native land. [Applause.] They found in this country the democratic party ever ready to defend them in the exercise of these rights, and they will ever sustain this party, whether bull-bruised or not. [Applause.] But the Irish citizens of this country have rights, and they will sustain them. It was to organize an association for the purpose of defending these rights, and seeing that a proper representation of Irishmen was had upon the tickets at the approaching election, that this meeting was called. He moved that a committee be appointed to nominate permanent officers of the association. Carried, and the chair appointed the following gentlemen as such committee: Thomas Gallagher, Patrick Shanahan, Jeremiah Calnon, Patrick Gallagher and Patrick Ratigan.

On motion of Mr. Thos. Howrigan a committee of one from each ward was appointed by the meeting to draft resolutions, as follows:

First Ward, Mark McGraw; Second Ward, Patrick McGinnis; Third Ward, Phillip Sutton; Fourth Ward, Miles J. O'Reilly; Fifth Ward, Thos. W. Cooper; Sixth Ward, George H. Nesbitt; Seventh Ward, James McGonnegal; Eighth Ward, William Purcell; Ninth Ward, James O'Connor; Tenth Ward, Thomas C. Fitzgibbon.

The committee on permanent organization reported the following officers:

President:—Hugh Flynn.

Vice Presidents—John Collins, Patrick McGin-

Figure 7 – Political activism of the Irish in Detroit. SOURCE: May 10, 1860; ProQuest Historical Newspapers: Detroit Free Press, pg.1

Knights of Equity.

The Knights of Equity (K of E), an Irish Catholic fraternal organization, was established in 1895 with the Detroit Court 6 early among its 65 branches, organizing in 1896. They donated their clubhouse at Fort and Second to the University of Detroit in 1924. Their initial goals were non-discrimination, equal rights, and financial security of Irish-Americans, and this gave force to its social and philanthropic emphasis.

During its period of greatest influence, the K of E was an important Catholic society. It evolved with the times, creating a sister arm for women, called the Daughters of Erin. Today, just three branches remain, in Detroit, Pittsburgh and Buffalo.

Society of the Friendly Sons of St. Patrick for the Relief of Emigrants of Ireland.

The Friendly Sons were formed specifically to aid the Irish emigrant, as the official organization name suggests, and they trace their roots to 1771 in one of the oldest European settlements in America, colonial Philadelphia. As such, they are actually older than the AOH.

Rather than a militant defender, like the AOH, the Friendly Sons has been a welfare organization, preoccupied for a century with Irish starvation and exile. They organized the St Patrick's Alliance of America in 1868 to provide sick and death benefits for Catholic Irish, much as the mutual aid societies did when introducing insurance. By the late 19th century, they were aiding disaster victims, from the Jonestown Pennsylvania flood, to the San Francisco earthquake, to victims of the Spanish-American War and the 1916 Irish uprising.

The organization has expanded to focus on encouraging "greater interest in ties of friendship between America and Ireland", and today sponsors scholarships and educational endowments.

Gaelic League.

Another Irish organization that was mainly nationalist, non-partisan and non-sectarian in outlook was formed in order to combat increasing Anglicization of Ireland in the late 19th century. Three aims of the Gaelic League, formed in Dublin in July 1893, were honored among expatriates in the United States:

- preservation of Irish as the national language of Ireland and promotion of it as a spoken language
- study and publication of existing Gaelic literature
- cultivation of a modern literature in Irish.

The Gaelic Revival of the 19th century may be the only reason anything about Ireland's culture or language is known today. English domination had pushed Gaelic culture to the point of extinction until scholars began to organize and advocate for preservation of literature, language and sporting traditions. In 1884, the Gaelic Athletic Association (GAA) was founded, and hurling and Gaelic football were played throughout Ireland.

> "While it would have seemed unlikely that the Irish language would prove to be a unifying force among the American Irish given its progressive decline in postfamine Ireland, allied to other aspects of nationality within the American context, it acquired a significant import in Irish-American organizations. And in the Irish quest for assimilation to the host country, a badge of ethnicity that indicated an ancient and glorious past rather than a demeaned and debased one could prove invaluable. An accurate analysis of the Irish community in the New World needs to recognize that there was also a flowering of cultural consciousness and debate among the Irish in the United States in the closing decades of the nineteenth century. This led to the creation of a unique Irish cultural identity in the United States."
>
> *Úna Ní Bhroiméil, "The Creation of an Irish Culture in the United States: The Gaelic Movement, 1870-1915"*

As the cultural movement caught on, Irish scholar Douglas Hyde (who would become first president of Ireland in 1938) urged, "We must teach ourselves not to be ashamed of ourselves, because the Gaelic people can never produce its best before the world as long as it remains tied to the apron-strings of another race and another island." One year after his speech, the Gaelic League was founded in Dublin, creating newspapers and other works written in Gaelic. Many members of the GAA, the Gaelic League and literary societies became key members of the Irish nationalist movement.

Figure 8 – Translated as "The Flaming Sword," this was the Gaelic language paper of the international Gaelic League. SOURCE: Public Domain. Accessed from www.cng.ie/en/info/22-a-brief-history-of-the-conradh.html

"League of the Gaels - Country and Tongue". SOURCE: Public Domain, Accessed from www.cnag.ie/en/membership/25-english-bearla/info/conradh-na-gaeilge/22-a-brief-history-of-the-conradh.html

According to Irish Central magazine, Irish Americans came to play a critical role in the Gaelic revival. 1.5 million Irish came to American between 1880 and 1910, a quarter from counties with 40% or more Gaelic speakers. Irish communities in America published newspapers and literary journals in Gaelic, so that the Freeman's Journal, one of Ireland's oldest newspapers, commented in 1883 that Irish-Americans seemed more interested in the Irish language than those in Ireland. The bilingual monthly journal, An Gaodhal, sold 2,880 copies monthly in America in 1882 while the Gaelic Journal in Dublin had only 400 subscribers. (Wertz, 2016).

By 1903, 600 Gaelic League branches organized language classes and initiated debates and lectures through "An Claidheamh Soluis" (the flaming sword).

> Language was looked upon as the most fundamental part of self-image and self-definition in relation to the natural and social environment, the collective memory and the carrier of the native worldview. In addition, the Gaelic League also stressed in their constitution that their mission was non-political; in no small part to the divisive nature of Irish politics. As well as attempting to bring Catholics and Protestants together, it was also hoped that this notion of inclusivity would eliminate unwanted political attention.
>
> SOURCE: "Irish History Live," School of History and Anthropology, Queen's University Belfast. www.qub.ac.uk/sites/irishhistorylive/IrishHistoryResources/Shortarticlesandencyclopaediaentries/Encyclopaedia/LengthyEntries/GaelicLeague/

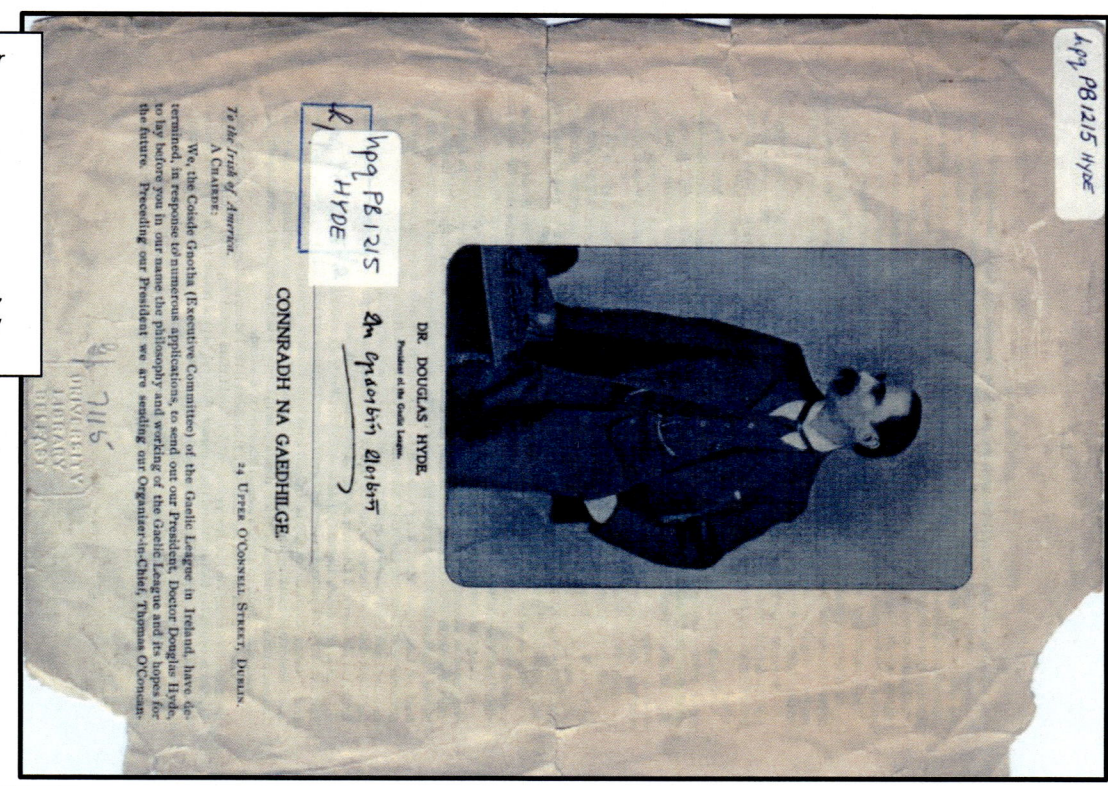

Figure 9 – "A letter to the Irish of America from the Executive Committee", Dublin, 1905, p.2.

SOURCE: Special Collections Library, Queen's University Belfast.

Modern Irish cultural centers.

A new generation of ethnic-oriented gathering places have been built since the 1970s, with a broader and more public facing scope and larger and more deliberate in design. These places are cultural centers combining purposes of the old social clubs, with newer functions such as research, education, museum and artistic installations, and facility rentals.

The centers differ from the old clubs in several ways:

- Tax deductible status for donors taps the growing philanthropy sector and the general public, with the result that much of the calendar is not focused on fraternization
- Business ventures may be profit-focused, and management and operations professionalized
- They are often campus settings, and thus larger and apart from a city neighborhood or from a residential base
- Designers craft user experiences, rather than users defining the space (or space being ill-defined)

Some prominent examples of these multi-purpose cultural centers include:

1. **Cleveland Westside Irish Cultural Center, opened 1972**. The organization started as a social club in 1931 and moved about various homes and shared halls in the Irish enclave from W.64th to W.74th street, until acquiring their own storefront (now operated as Cleveland Public Theater). As club leaders perceived urban change in the 1960s, they shopped for suburban land for a new facility and acquired 26 acres in the westside suburb of Olmsted Falls. The new location not only has a hall and meeting rooms, but large landscaped grounds including a gazebo, pavilion and a lake ideal for their traditional annual picnic as well as special events and private celebrations.

2. **Chicago's Irish-American Heritage center, opened 1985.** The 501.c.3 charitable organization is focused on Irish cultural education through programming. They opened in a former school and now operate a Library, museum, art gallery, archives, classrooms, performance center, pub and gift shop. Well known to celebrities and foreign dignitaries, the center houses the Irish hall of fame.

3. **Phoenix's Irish Cultural Center and McClelland Library, opened in** 2001. A relatively recent addition to the landscape, the campus was built entirely with funds raised by the Irish Cultural and Learning Foundation, then donated to the municipal government of Phoenix. The Foundation administers the various programs, classes, festivals and special events including history, music, art, dance, literature, drama, crafts, language, travel and sports.

The McClelland Library was designed by architect, Paul Ahern, after a 12th century Norman Castle, and another building invokes the old stone cottages of the Irish countryside. The three-story building, largest of its kind in the western U.S., houses 8,000 books from Irish authors, poets, and genealogical sources. The library houses a permanent exhibit on The Book of Kells, reading rooms, and computer access to disciplines of Irish and Celtic studies.

4. **Irish Cultural Centre of New England, opened 1989**. The 43-acre campus in West Springfield Massachusetts has the mission of fostering a connection to Ireland, and they have relationships with educational and cultural institutions in Ireland and serve as an advocate for international exchange students and other Irish immigrants.

    The center has a collection of literature, film and art and archives that draws the broad New England region. A full calendar of events ranges from performances and classroom instruction to cultural festivals and speakers on international relations. Services also include the Irish House Restaurant and Trinity Pub.

5. **United Irish Cultural Center of San Francisco, opened 1985**. Built entirely by volunteer labor and community donations not far from the Pacific Ocean, the organization is a 501.c.3 charitable nonprofit with an educational mission. The facility has a library and performance venue, it offers programming including everything from

live arts performances to set dancing classes to Gaelic Athletic Association viewing parties, and it hosts special event rentals.

DID ETHNIC CLUBS UNITE OR DIVIDE?

Ethnic clubs provided invaluable services to vulnerable ethnic populations, but they also reinforced their identities as disadvantaged. "Ethnicization of consciousness", according to Jonathan Sarna, meant that some people became even more aware of their ethnicity, and set in their own ways, as a result of ethnic-focused organizations. Ethnic populations arrived to the new land person by person or family by family; later, they bonded and united around aspects of their native culture, often in consequence of traits ascribed to them or of adversities faced in the new environment.

A widely held view has these social clubs playing an important role in assimilation of new arrivals to America. Many learned the language and customs, found work, and raised kids under the umbrella of these organizations. They supported practices like parades or choirs that introduced cherished cultural traditions into broad acceptance. Foreign people were eased into American life. Assimilation was critical to the largest economic expansion and most dramatic political rise of a nation in history.

Today, ethnic social clubs are not only a source of heritage for members, but a celebration of the diverse core of America's urban places. Ethnic clubs highlight the variety of ingredients that shaped American life and ascendance. These organizations enjoy broad patronage outside of their factions, and those that continue to operate their historic clubhouses evoke nostalgia and support for the historic urban centers in which they reside.

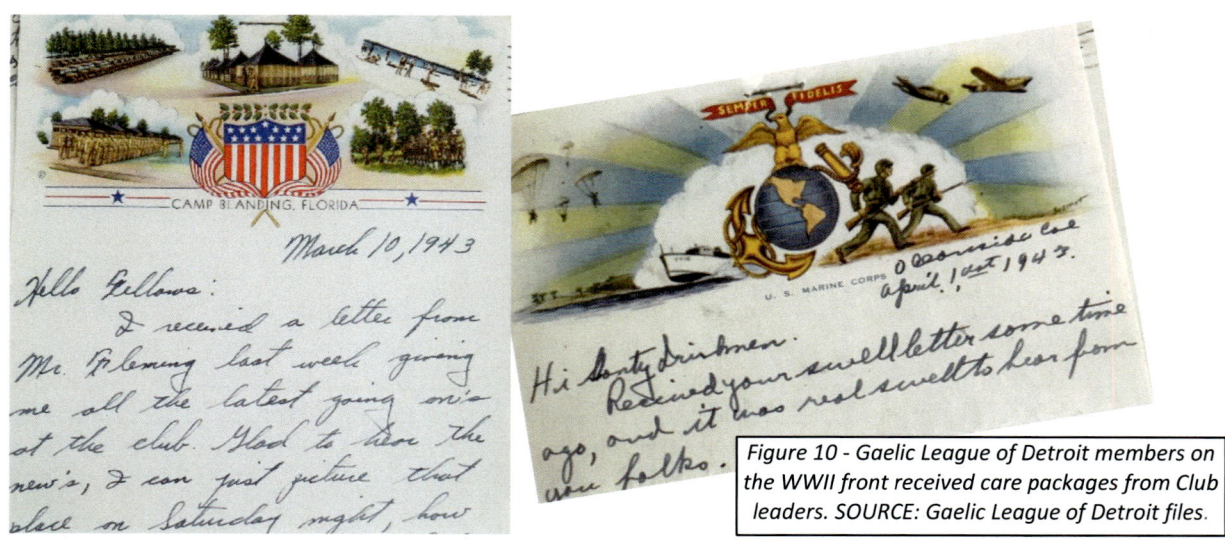

Figure 10 - Gaelic League of Detroit members on the WWII front received care packages from Club leaders. SOURCE: Gaelic League of Detroit files.

FRATERNAL ETHNIC CLUBS TODAY

Few ethnic social clubs operate their historic clubhouses in 21st century America. Many clubs dissolved without subsequent generations of immigrants needing benevolent aid, or descendants of immigrants celebrating cultural traditions. People moved and assimilated.

The stalwarts still operating their historic clubhouses have reinvented the social club for a new generation that is more mobile and has more leisure opportunities. These new establishments are celebrated as evidence of their city's heritage of diversity and America's history of immigration. Their clubhouses are part of the city's urban identity and they anchor historic corridors. They are not commercial in nature, and they bring people together.

Baltimore's Arch Social Club. 2426 Pennsylvania Avenue, at North Avenue, West Baltimore.

Founded in 1905, the Arch Social Club may be the oldest operating African-American social club. In the strictly segregated Baltimore of the turn of the last century, its mere existence was a challenge to Jim Crow, seeking "The social, moral, and intellectual uplift of its members." Some African-American organizations would choose members based on skin tone, social class, religious or political affiliation, but Arch had professionals and longshoremen and labor organizers. Some club members followed the teachings of Booker T. Washington, some have been Marcus Garvey militants, and still others were W.E.B. DuBois devotees.

As a whole, African-Americans lacked financial or political resources to invest in clubhouses, so the Arch is special for this reason as well. Brother Kaleb Tshambe, Arch Club historian, argues that Baltimore's Pennsylvania Avenue is as important to African-American history as is Harlem. In the 1920s and '30s, some of the country's first right-to-work boycotts occurred there. By the '50s, when natives Billie Holiday and Cab Calloway performed at black-owned movie theaters and jazz clubs, and the Arch had more than 200 active members, limousines were a common sight. The building was not purchased until 1972.

Figure 11 – ABOVE: Artist Ernest Shaw's mural "Sankofa", unveiled on the north façade in 2015. SOURCE: Arch Social Club, Ronald Hollie.

LEFT: façade restored in 2013. SOURCE: www.explore.baltimoreheritage.org/items/show/331

Buffalo's Adam Mickiewicz Library and Dramatic Circle. 612 Fillmore Avenue, Historic Polonia District.

Figure 12 – *When the flag is out, the club is open.* SOURCE: www.ForgottenBuffalo.com

In 1895, an employee of a Polish newspaper in Buffalo's Polish section gathered 15 influential Polish immigrants to form a circle of cultural activities for Polish youth. They were offered space in St Stanislaus, formed the decade prior, and they began producing amateur theatre shows.

Membership grew so quickly that they found a building on Fillmore Avenue, blocks away, and built a bar, theatre and meeting rooms in 1914. The club has been a center for Polish nationals, their children learning their Polish heritage, and immigrants fleeing wartime communism. It was a center for political engagement in the turbulent '60s.

The heart of Buffalo's historic polish area, the 12,000 volume library includes 400 hand copied plays. The bar offers dozens of imported beers. The 1000-year old Dyngus Day tradition marks the end of Lenten abstinence with parades, polka, food and drink and other fun traditions.

Cleveland's Bohemian National Hall, Home of Sokol Greater Cleveland Czech Cultural Center. 4939 Broadway, Slavic Village neighborhood.

Cleveland Bohemian National Hall cornerstone was laid in 1896 as a community hall to accommodate the cultural, social, and educational needs of Czech immigrants. The multistory brick building was built on the eastside of the industrial valley, in the center of the city's concentration of Slavic immigrants.

"Sokol," the promotion of moral values through physical education, was formulated in 1862 by Dr Miroslav Tyrs, a professor who created calisthenics, and by Jindrich Fugner in the Austrian Czech lands (which would become Czechoslovakia and now the Czech Republic and the Slovak Republic). Like German Turnerism, the program was based on the democratic principles of ancient Greeks to develop "a sound mind in a sound body", as only physically fit, mentally alert, and culturally developed citizens can make a nation strong and patriotic. Sokol also went to St Louis (1865), Chicago (1866), New York (1867) and Baltimore (1872).

The hall was the locus of advocacy for the homeland. Representatives for the Czech and Slovak people met there in 1915 to discuss a common sovereign state. The Cleveland Agreement sparked the idea of what would come to be Czechoslovakia in 1945. The hall celebrated the liberation of Czechoslovakia from German occupation, with speeches by presidents of the Slovak National Alliance and the Czechoslovakian Consul. Leaders called for unity among

Czechs and Poland, Hungary, and Austria, and held clothing and household goods drives for war-torn Czechoslovakia.

In 1975, Bohemian National Hall was added to the National Register of Historic Places, then, sold to American Sokol Inc. The hall continues to host Sokol meetings, gymnastic events, and lodge functions, even as the surrounding area has have emptied.

Figure 13 – view of Bohemian National Hall and Broadway Avenue includes plaza sculpture PHOTO: google earth

Gaelic League Irish American Club of Detroit. 2068 Michigan Ave, Corktown neighborhood.

Figure 14 – The lounge area evokes the traditional Irish hearth. PHOTO: author 2019.

Generations after the largest wave of Irish immigration in Detroit, a group of twenty men gathered downtown to form the Gaelic League of Detroit. The Club has a two-tiered membership structure, with Gaelic League members voted in on basis of Irish ancestry and volunteer effort, and Irish American membership for casual and social members. The organization's daily operations are led by volunteers, and it maintains over 800 members.

Michigan Avenue is one of the five arterial "spokes" of Detroit's road pattern, and the clubhouse is in the three prominent blocks surrounding the historic 1912 Michigan Central Train Station which Ford Motor Company is developing. Ford's plans for the Beaux Arts landmark have bolstered a significant period of reinvestment in Detroit's oldest neighborhood, and much interest in the club's future.

The Irish have a long history of community organization, and the Gaelic League is part of a web of Irish-American organizations dedicated to irish welfare and heritage in metropolitan Detroit. These organizations include the Knights of Equity, Ancient Order of Hibernians, Fraternal Order of United Irishmen, and United Irish Societies with whom they collaborate to put on the annual St. Patrick's Day parade. They are a number of cultural nonprofit groups as well, with whom they have formed a consortium to assure broader appreciation of Irish cultural programming: Detroit Irish Musicians Association, Detroit Irish Radio, Irish Cultural Forum, Irish Genealogy Society of Michigan, Irish Language Circle, Kitty's Ceili and the Brunch Program. The Gaelic League is the center of metro Detroit's Irish community.

Milwaukee's Turnverein in Turner Hall. 1034 North 4th Street, Westown Downtown.
Philadelphia's Roxborough Turners. 418 Leverington Ave, Roxborough.
Cleveland's Eastside Turners. E. 55th Street, Superior-St Clair section.

The Milwaukee Turners (1855), Philadelphia's Roxborough Turners (1873), and Cleveland's Eastside Turners (1908) have their roots in the German Turnverein associations founded in 1811 to prepare youth to fight against Napoleonism. These clubs are shells of the hundreds of Turnverein societies existing in 19th century America.

The Turnverein traditionally focused on the mental and physical, as tools to resist anti-democratic forms of government. In the United States, German immigrants created vigorous athletic, cultural, and social societies with the Turner motto, "Sound Mind in a Sound Body," and they lobbied for physical education in the public schools. Turners promoted vigorous civic engagement.

Their holistic vision commits to free speech, free press, and free assembly so that men and women may order their lives by dictates of conscience:

> "Liberty, against all oppression;
> Tolerance, against all fanaticism;
> Reason, against all superstition;
> Justice, against all exploitation."

Milwaukee's Turners have opened a trust for preservation of the four-story High Victorian masonry building, now used as a

Figure 15 – Philadelphia's Roxborough Turners clubhouse. PHOTO: google earth

performance venue and clubhouse, 70 years after finances had driven them from the fire damaged building.

Turner Hall's front facade has projecting gabled sections near its corners, and a central entrance deeply recessed under another gable which rises to a five-story pyramid-capped tower. The interior includes a ballroom with balcony, restaurant and beer hall, meeting room, and modern gymnasium in the basement. The interior includes rare murals by German immigrant artists and stained glass windows with progressive political slogans. The building was completed in 1882 (addition, 1899).

Cleveland's Eastside Turners today only operate their historic gymnasium in Cleveland's St Clair-Superior section, and Philadelphia's Roxborough Turners have a lower profile as well.

Figure 16 – Historic hall modernization
SOURCE: google earth

Figure 17 – PHOTO: unknown, public domain. Accessed through Wikimedia attributed to James Steakley file (George Brosius, "Fifty Years Devoted to the Cause of Physical Culture, 1864-1914, Milwaukee: Germania Publishing, 1914). www.commons.wikimedia.org/wiki/File:Milwaukee Bundesturnhalle.jpg.

Philadelphia's Palizzi Social Club. 1408 South 12th Street, Passyunk Square.

The Italian Mafia is a cliché today, but numerous social clubs in New York and Philadelphia at the turn of the last century were so exclusive that Italians from only one "Old Country" region could join. These places hosted anniversaries, funerals, business deals and parties.

With major Italian immigration in the 19th and early 20th centuries, South Philly was home to several Italian social clubs and still houses the popular ten block Italian Market of S. 9th Street. The last of these clubs is the Palizzi Social Club. When founded in 1918, only expats from the town of Vasto could join; the club took its name from the town's most famous resident, painter Filippo Palizzi. Over the years, it expanded to include a family related to the original owners.

Palizzi food and dining rules (palizzisocial.com):

Members Only | Cash Only
No loud obnoxious behavior
Proper attire required
Gentlemen must remove hats, and no flip-flops or sweatpants are allowed
Do not linger outside the front stoop
Smokers can use the backyard
What happens at Palizzi stays at Palizzi
No pictures or excessive cell phone use
No blogging, reviewing, tagging on social media
Each member may bring three non-members
If you wouldn't bring them to your mom's house, don't bring them here
A membership does not guarantee entry
Please have patience when we are at capacity
Exit briskly and silently
Our neighbors are sleeping next door
Eat a lot, drink more, and mostly: be social

Figure 18 – Simple, private, nondescript clubhouse. Photo: google earth

Pittsburgh's Teutonia Mannerchor. 859 Phineas, Deutchtown neighborhood.

The heart of Teutonia Mannerchor is the traditional men's choir, for which the club is named. The choir rehearse traditional German songs in the hall on the second floor of its 1884 clubhouse in the Deutchtown section on Pittsburgh's north shore. The men's choir and a more recently formed ladies choir compete at national conventions whose championship tapestries adorn the hall in glass enclosures.

In the basement of the split-level structure, members socialize in a rathskeller accented by murals. Rathskeller (or "ratskeller") in German-speaking countries refers to a bar located in a basement of a city hall. The concept has been popular in American cities since the 19th century, as has the German beer garden ("biergarten"). Steins from annual Strong Man contests date to the Plague, and pegs behind the 1930's updated bar hold steins of members, under a ledge with steins of the deceased. The Club is landscaping its grounds into a beer garden for special or seasonal events.

Members still recite the creed written when Teutonia Mannerchor was formed in 1854. "We constitute a society whose aim is to further choral singing, German cultural tradition and good fellowship. We require each member to co-operate and assist us in this endeavor in every way." With 2700 members today, that aim is solid.

Figure 19 – Clubhouse and grounds (RIGHT) and front entrance (ABOVE) in Deutschtown, Pittsburgh.

PHOTOS: google earth

Pittsburgh's John Kollar Literary and Library Society (1913). 3226 Jane Street, The Hollow neighborhood.

John Kollar Literary and Library Society of Pittsburgh formed to teach English to Slovakian immigrants streaming into the city for mining and mill jobs. Tucked into the last residential block of The Hollow, at the edge of the south side slopes off the old industrial waterfront, the modest storefront with the Slovakian flag fits with its two-story wood frame neighbors. The backyard is a postage stamp of grass in the dense residential block, and a narrow sliver of alley parks cars.

Its ambition a century ago was anything but modest – seeking literacy for members, so they could be self-sufficient in their new home. Hence, the great Slovakian literary figure John Kollar as its namesake. The club became a place of news about the troubled motherland. Their creed reflected their citizenship: "To cultivate raising moral standards and education among Slovak youths and Americans of Slovak descent."

The Pittsburgh region has the largest concentration of Slovakians outside of the small central European country of 5 million, with nearly ¼ million of Slovakian descent. In 1905 alone, 50,000 migrated from the poverty and oppression of repeated occupation. The club remains a mix of Charter members and social members, with a schedule of events and language classes.

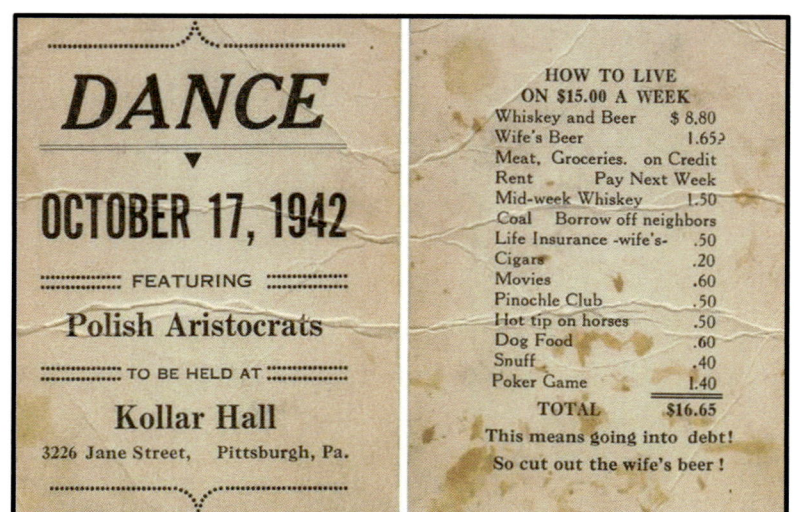

Figure 20 – Kollar Club Event program (LEFT) SOURCE: https://newsinteractive.post-gazette.com/thedigs/2013/07/31/pittsburghs-kollar-club/

BELOW: Kollar Club logo

San Francisco's Polish Club (1894), 3040 S. 22nd Street. South side.

California's Polish population started actively organizing in the 1860s, and cultural and charitable efforts soon followed. Formation of San Francisco's Polish Club early in the 20th century is a case study in organizing.

The Polish National Congress was established first in San Francisco, and it became an early provider of life insurance for Polish Californians. The Literary and Dramatic Circle was established to arrange recitals, lectures and book-clubs of Polish literary works and it promoted careers of local Poles in literary or other artistic fields. The St Stanislaus Benevolent Society was formed to support Polish religious and educational efforts. After Poland won national independence in the Great War, these three organizations came together in what was then California's biggest city in order to collect funds to send home, and in 1926 these three groups became founding members of the Polish Club in San Francisco.

Figure 21 – Unassuming Club entrance on S. 22nd Street. PHOTO: google earth

The Polish Club converted a church to a clubhouse to provide gathering space for new arrivals. It was a social club and it arranged insurance and other mutual aid. The emergence of the Polish National Congress meant, according to scholar John Bodnar, "immigrants would learn a fundamental fact about surviving in a modern industrial society, namely, security could be better pursued through large scale organizations rather than through small groups." The modest frame structure still resides in the heart of a residential neighborhood in the industrial southside of the city.

San Francisco Italian Athletic Club (1917), 1630 Stockton, North Beach neighborhood.

Located across from historic Saints Peter and Paul church, overlooking Washington Square in the Little Italy/North Beach section, the club is ideally situated to be the heart of San Francisco's Italian community. Washington Square is San Francisco's first city park (1847) and the church, destroyed in the earthquake and fire of 1906, was rebuilt spectacularly.

The club has a bar and gym for members-only use, and a ballroom and balcony area for formal events for the community. The monthly stag dinner is its most traditional feature, and its hold as a men-only club is so strong that women finally formed their own club in 2010, La Donne D'Italia, which operates out of the same facility as the 650+ member men's club.

The building was completed in 1936, a decade after the merger of several local Italian clubs. They host the annual Italian American Parade and Dinner every Fall, the Festa Coloniale, an annual outdoor music festival in Washington Square, and the 100-year old "Statuto" or open foot race throughout the city. As an athletic club, they host an annual Bocce tournament and a golf tournament, in addition to sponsoring competitive soccer and cycling teams. Their beginner and conversational Italian classes are popular.

Figure 22 – Stockton Avenue façade, from Washington Square. PHOTO: google earth

FRATERNAL ORGANIZATIONS OPERATING HISTORIC CLUBHOUSES IN DETROIT TODAY

The heyday of the fraternal organization left an indelible imprint on cities, and a number of these historic organizations continue to operate in Detroit today. The landscape has changed, and the organizations have transformed their legal and operating structures. Some no longer operate as fraternal organizations, or no longer operate their historic clubhouses. Some have survived as fraternal organizations with the business, educational or recreational focus intact.

Two of the twelve surviving fraternal clubs in Detroit are ethnic social clubs: the Maltese American Benevolent Society operates within blocks of the Gaelic League of Detroit, on Michigan Avenue in the Corktown neighborhood, where their respective populations had originally resided.

Historic Fraternal Organizations Operating Historic Facilities in Detroit

Fraternal Organization	When Formed	Historic Clubhouse (when acquired)	Distinction
Detroit Boat Club Crew	1839	E. Picnic Way, Belle Isle (1902)	Friends of Detroit Rowing 501.c.3 to restore boathouse
Detroit Yacht Club	1868	1 Riverbank Road, Belle Isle (1922)	501.c.3 conservancy for building
Detroit Club	1882	702 Cass Ave (1891)	Reopened with public amenities
Detroit Athletic Club	1887	251 Madison (1915)	501.c.3 foundation for building
Yondotega Club	1891	1450 E. Jefferson (1959)	Shrouded in mystery as to membership and activities
Detroit Golf Club	1899	17911 Hamilton (1918)	Foundation for scholarships
Indian Village Tennis Club	1912	1502 Parker (1912)	Small and volunteer-operated
Bayview Yacht Club	1915	100 Clairpointe (1928)	Foundation supports annual showpiece Mackinaw Race
Gaelic League of Detroit	1920	2068 Michigan (1951)	Cultural consortium
Kappa Alpha Psi Fraternity, Detroit Alumni Chapter	1920	259 Erskine (1945)	Artifacts in Smithsonian
Omega Psi Phi Fraternity, Nu Omega Chapter	1923	235 E. Ferry (1942)	Charitable Friends arm formed
Maltese American Benevolent Society	1940	1832 Michigan (1963)	Detroit post WWII had largest concentration of Maltese

Figure 23 – Author's analysis, based on IRS Code 501c.7 filings, accessed through propublica.org

A POWERFUL LEGACY STILL EVIDENT IN DETROIT'S BUILDING STOCK.

The architectural legacy of the private club era is on display in Detroit. A few of the finest remains in 2020 include:

- Oddfellows building on Randolph and Gratiot
- Masonic Temple, the largest in the world when built at the foot of Cass
- the 15-story Knights of the Maccabees building in the cultural center
- Deutsch Haus on Mack at Seminole
- Grand Army of the Republic castle near the foot of Grand River
- Wayne Order of the Amaranth, Gratiot and McDougall at Preston
- Loyal Order of the Moose Lodge at Cass and Elizabeth downtown
- former German Harmonie Club at 267 E. Harmonie
- Dom Polski halls on Junction near St Hedwig and on E. Forest at Chene Street

These buildings long survive the clubs that enlivened the 19th and early 20th century, when fraternal organizations had their heyday throughout the country. Their namesakes in many cases continue to rest high on the building facades. Other buildings are lost, either to replacement by a larger and grander structure befitting the City's ascent, as happened with the first Maccabees building, or to the dissolution of the organization, as happened to the Ancient Order of Gleaners.

Figure 24 – FAR LEFT: Odd Fellows Building at Randolph and Gratiot. TOP RIGHT: Deutsch Haus headquarters on Mack Avenue. SOURCE: Author, 2019

BOTTOM RIGHT: Ancient Order of Gleaners clubhouse, once on Woodward Avenue, circa 1910.

SOURCE: Detroit Publishing Company

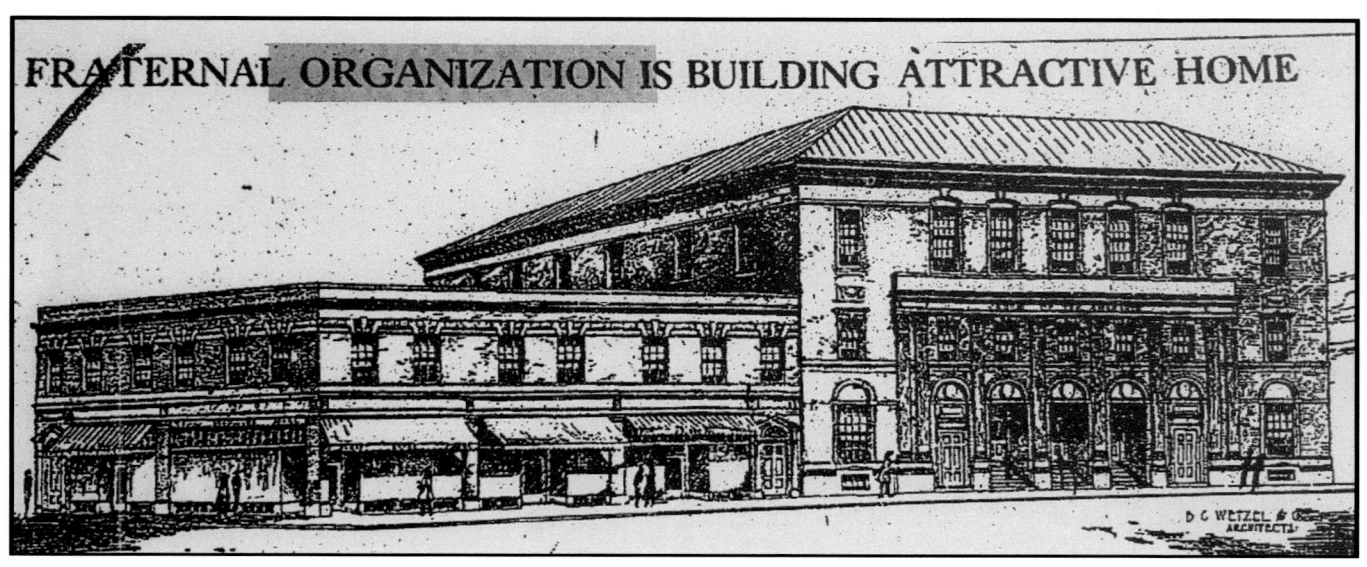

Figure 25 – Building for Wayne Assembly, Order of the Amaranth, on Gratiot. "Fraternal Organization is Building Attractive Home" Detroit Free Press (1858-1922): Nov 27, 1921. SOURCE: ProQuest Historical Newspapers, Detroit Free Press p.20.

Figure 26 – First Knights of the Maccabees organization clubhouse on Woodward Avenue, circa 1905, which was replaced in 1927 by a 15-story skyscraper just north of Warren Avenue.

SOURCE: Detroit Publishing Company glass negative

Detroit Boat Club Crew (1839). E. Picnic Way, Belle Isle Park.

The Detroit Boat Club is the oldest social rowing club in North America. When founded in 1839, Detroit had not yet developed industry nor expanded from its downtown core. Its mission is to promote rowing throughout Metro Detroit, which it does today through the Friends of Detroit Rowing, a 501c3 organization, and out of its 1902 Mediterranean Clubhouse marking the entrance to Belle Isle Park.

The club reorganized several times in its two centuries but continues to provide competitive and recreational programs for men and women of all ages and abilities. This includes training for rowers competing on national, international, and Olympic levels. 2019 marks the 125th Annual Sailing Regatta on Lake Saint Clair, and the organizations continue to reinvest in the historic clubhouse and dock facilities.

Figure 27 – Veranda of the 1902 Detroit Boat Club headquarters. SOURCE: Detroit Publishing Company

Detroit Yacht Club (1868). 1 Riverbank Road, Belle Isle Park.

Men of leisure in early Detroit found their way to the river, and boating clubs were among the first formed. The first clubhouses were modest and functional, and the Detroit Yacht Club's (DYC's) first clubhouse met the fate familiar to the times and burned. Three more ever-larger clubhouses followed.

As Detroit boomed in the 1920s, the DYC built an architectural wonder befitting a world city. At a $1 million cost, the 93,000 sq.ft. Mediterranean Villa was designed by famed architect George Mason, on its own island contiguous to the public island park, with a 100-year lease from the City. In 2011, the structure was placed on the National Register of Historic Places, and a 501.c.3 charitable foundation was formed to assure preservation of the building, its paintings, tapestries and historic trophies, and to promote enjoyment by the public.

The DYC, as its famed burgee calls it, remains the largest yacht club in the nation in arguably the most unique location. Membership peaked at over 3000 and 350 boat wells surround its island site. In 1924, the club began to sponsor the Hydroplane races on the river and gained international attention. The club thrived and expanded the river vista, adding an Olympic pool and movie watching facilities.

Figure 28 – Detroit Yacht Club, early headquarters building on Belle Isle Park.

SOURCE: Detroit Publishing Company

Detroit Club (1882, reorganized 2018). 702 Cass Avenue.

Inside the 4-story brick and stone Detroit Club is a formal mantel, four bowling alleys, a library, dining rooms, billiard parlor, barbershop, wine cellar, café and private rooms for members. The impressive architectural façade hosted many significant landmark events in auto industry history: formation of the influential Automobile Club of Detroit in 1902; Henry Ford II's negotiations with Harry Bennett for sole control of Ford Motor Company; even Chrysler CEO Lee Iacocca's campaign to restore the Statue of Liberty and build the Ellis Island Museum started here.

The re-booted club offers premium sporting event tickets, valet service, wine lockers and a spa and exercise space. A rooftop bar signals its commitment to Detroit's ongoing revitalization, as does its preservation of period details.

Figure 29 – Detroit Club entrance on Cass and Fort in downtown Detroit. SOURCE: Author, October 2019

Figure 30 – Detroit Club Ballroom (right) and bar (below). SOURCE: Author, October 2019.

Detroit Athletic Club (1887, reorganized in 1913). 251 Madison Avenue.

Detroit's leading citizens established this club on a national wave of interest in athletics, in 1887. As a new class of industrial leaders emerged in 1913, the club was re-booted and pre-eminent architect Albert Kahn was commissioned for a larger and more prominent design. Most of the 130 new Detroit Athletic Club members added after the new clubhouse opened were auto industry leaders, and combined with the outstanding architecture, the club made national news.

Figure 31 – First Detroit Athletic Club headquarters, circa 1900. SOURCE: Detroit Publishing Company

The magnificent six-story clubhouse which they operate today is a mainstay of the city's historic theatre district on and around Madison Avenue. The sculptures, paintings and Brussels tapestries alone would distinguish the building. But there is marble trim, oak paneling and arched and gilded ceilings, as well as chandeliers, frescoes and fireplaces throughout the variety of rooms. The club has a full calendar and lunch and formal dinner restaurants.

Yondotega Club (1891). 1450 East Jefferson Avenue.

Some of Detroit's biggest business names are linked to its most mysterious club: Alger, Briggs, Buhl, Fisher, Ford, to name a few of Detroit's leading 20th century business figures. The original riverfront site of the Yondotega Club was lost to the development of interstate 375 in the early 1960s, and it now occupies a brick clubhouse sitting behind brick walls tucked into the obscurity of East Jefferson's modern mix. The small organization filed its public record tax form in 2018 with $673,000 of annual income.

The building of their new site gave the rare glimpse into the private club's workings. A *Detroit Times* article of the period revealed of the 100 member-limited club that no business was allowed to be discussed at the site; no woman and no non-member Wayne County resident had ever set foot inside; and few outside guests were ever entertained with the notable exception of former President Theodore Roosevelt in 1926. They were sentimental enough to replant finials from the original club, and to relocate the glass-enclosed pergola in which card games were played to the new site. A crystal chandelier donated by Henry Ford II was installed amid various memorial plaques and decorations.

Figure 32 – entrance from E. Jefferson SOURCE: Google earth

Detroit Golf Club (1899). 17911 Hamilton.

Located in the most exclusive residential section of northwest Detroit, not far from the University of Detroit Mercy, the Detroit Golf Club retains an aura of vintage Detroit while drawing from the sprawling metropolitan area.

The Club is so accomplished today that it hosts a Professional Golf Association (PGA) tournament. The organization was started with 6 holes and 100 members, and it has expanded several times to its present size of 36 holes and 650-member limit. The expansions have added tennis courts, a caddy house, a pool and a crystal dining room sufficient to entertain an international audience.

The 36-hole course was designed by Donald Ross and the clubhouse by Albert Kahn. The Club has a resident pro, a swim team, and a scholarship program for its caddies through its charitable sister foundation.

Figure 33 – Detroit Golf Clubhouse, circa 1910.

SOURCE: Detroit Publishing Company glass negative.

Indian Village Tennis Club (1912). 1502 Parker Street.

Club facilities are located in the heart of one of Detroit's oldest and most prominent neighborhoods, in a private enclosure along Indian Village's west border. Despite recurring proposals to merge with other clubs and move to suburban locations, and a devastating fire in the clubhouse in 1984, the club has committed to staying in Detroit and operates three clay courts and a new, larger clubhouse with dining room, bar, commercial grade kitchen and locker rooms.

The Indian Village Tennis Club may be a modest and unassuming presence, but it has always been progressive in its inclusion policies, admitting women from the start, recognizing them as full "A" status members without playing restrictions in the 1970s, and electing an African-American President in 1983. Members have included Olympians and college stars in addition to neighborhood residents and prominent Detroiters.

Figure 34 – aerial view of the courts and clubhouse (upper left) in the Indian Village neighborhood. SOURCE: google earth

Bayview Yacht Club (1915). 100 Clairpointe Street.

A century of tradition in yacht racing and sailing instruction distinguishes the club whose members proudly say, "accomplishments on the water are more important than those off." Members have won signature races in the Atlantic Ocean, but the annual race from Port Huron to Mackinac Island is its showpiece, as its 1925 start makes it the longest continually run freshwater long distance sailboat race.

Members finished the clubhouse building piecemeal during the Great Depression. Before the clubhouse was completed, club members operated out of the affectionately nicknamed "Old Corrugated Iron Shack" next door to the women's swimming club and to a bootlegger's transfer point speakeasy.

Bayview Yacht Club has created a foundation to support the Mackinac Race, and it promotes racing, navigation and seamanship locally, nationally and internationally. Membership peaked in 2008 at 525 members. The club launched a major building campaign in 2019 to modernize its facilities for a younger audience.

Figure 35 - aerial view of Bayview Yacht Club grounds on the Detroit River, with clubhouse at the head. Maheras Gentry Park is left, and Conner Industrial Corridor foots to the west.

SOURCE: google earth.

Gaelic League Irish American Club of Detroit (1920). 2068 Michigan Avenue.

Detroit's Gaelic League is most known as the center of St Patrick's festivities every March. Thousands line Michigan Avenue in Corktown for the annual St Patrick's Parade, organized by a coalition of metropolitan Detroit Irish organizations convened by the United Irish Societies, and thousands pack the hall and grounds for Irish music and revelry on St Patrick's day. The clubhouse is host to charitable and neighborhood organizations in the 363 days per year it is open.

The Gaelic League originated as an advocate for the preservation of Irish culture. Answering the late 19th century worldwide call from academic Douglas Hyde (later to be President of the Irish Republic), Leagues formed around the world to keep alive Gaelic language and sporting traditions that were disappearing under English colonial rule. The Irish Language Circle continues to meet weekly at the Gaelic League of Detroit to "Speak the Irish." Live music, set dancing and ceili instruction are presented weekly, and the Irish Genealogical Society of Michigan meets monthly.

With its social affiliate, the Irish American Club, the organization celebrates Irish music and dance, language and heritage, public affairs, and presents whiskey, wine and beer tastings. Mayors, Governors and the President of Ireland have all been to the clubhouse, among other famous Irish.

*Figure 36 – RIGHT: 1931 Henry Ford letter to Irish Radio Hour.
BELOW: Rendering of Gaelic League clubhouse expansion, 1950.*

SOURCE: Gaelic League of Detroit files

Kappa Alpha Psi Fraternity, Inc – Historic Detroit Alumni Chapter (1920). 259 Erskine.

The Detroit Alumni Chapter of Kappa Alpha Psi Fraternity, Inc and the Kappa Detroit Foundation have been providing college scholarships and financial aid to young people in metro Detroit since 1920. These funds have made it possible for many academically deserving students to attend college who might not have otherwise been able.

The Board and membership body of the Kappa Detroit Foundation believe that those who have the opportunity for higher education are obligated to help the less fortunate. Early members included the distinguished Dr. Ossian H. Sweet, who had the unwelcomed fame of attacking white neighbors running him out of his Detroit home. In 1927, Detroit Alumni hosted the 17th Grand Chapter Meeting, and in 1945 unveiled the "Kappa Kastle" designed by architect Albert Kahn. 2014 Alumni donated fraternity memorabilia to the Smithsonian Museum.

Figure 37 - Clubhouse in Brush Park area. SOURCE: Author, Jan. 2020

Omega Psi Phi Fraternity, Inc., Nu Omega Chapter (1923). 235 E. Ferry Street.

The first international fraternal organization to be founded at an historically black college, in 1911, was at Howard University in Washington, D.C. Detroit's Nu Omega Chapter of the fraternity was chartered in 1923, and its Historic Omega House acquired in 1942 is one of the oldest continuously owned in the fraternity's history. Nu Omega is also one of the largest chapters in the fraternity.

Men of Nu Omega Chapter have several programs:

1. Scholarships for youth
2. Support of the Fine Arts (Talent Hunt Program)
3. Summer employment opportunities for youth
4. Thanksgiving and Christmas baskets for the underserved population of Detroit

Figure 38 – Clubhouse on E. Ferry, with State Historic registry plaque. PHOTO: Author, 2019.

Maltese American Benevolent Society (1940). 1832 Michigan Avenue.

Detroit's Maltese Club was a late arrival in the era of private fraternal organizations, but it has had staying power. The Michigan Avenue club, not far from the Gaelic League of Detroit, consists of a bar and lounge, large and small halls. It offers Maltese foods and treats such as Pastizzi, Rabbit Stew, Baked Rice and Macaroni and Figoli. Celebrations are family oriented and entertainment is day-long. The club has sponsored men's and co-ed soccer teams, but the main event is the Feast of The Virgin Mary. The club promotes the Maltese heritage, offering classes on Qassatat, as well as Brigoli and Figoli in preparation for Easter.

Figure 39 – Michigan Avenue location of the Maltese American Benevolent Society clubhouse.

SOURCE: google earth

WHAT FRATERNAL CLUBS ARE DOING TO ASSURE THEIR VITALITY

In the 21st century, historic fraternal organizations have reinvented themselves using 21st century tools. These organizations were internally focused and member-driven throughout their history, and they found themselves with migrating member bases and aging assets. The clubs had to maximize financial resources in order to offer a product meeting contemporary expectation.

Their historic assets now have wide appeal among non-members. There is broad interest in old cities and historic buildings, and there is curiosity about old forms of community. As a result, the clubs have adopted new forms of organization and processes to tap this interest and offset their liabilities.

Strategic Planning and Marketing of History.

Strategic plans set a long-term direction for an organization in order to leverage and focus resources. These organizations have history that is important in their field and in the city.

Fraternal ethnic clubs are special as noncommercial establishments where collective identity can be appreciated. They celebrate diversity and America's immigrant history. Their clubhouses are part of the history of the old urban center and sometimes are an anchor to their neighborhood communities. The plans capture this broad appeal.

Creating Trusts and Charitable 501c.3 Conservancies.

Charitable organizations have an advantage over fraternal organizations in fundraising. The IRS status provides tax deductibility for contributions to charitable organizations, per chapter and section 501.c.3. This status assures philanthropic foundations of the public benefit of their contributions. As a result, many clubs have formed as 501c.3.s to promote a heritage publically, but without the close alliances of the private club.

Many ethnic social clubs have lost their clubhouse because life is not very neighborhood-centered anymore. Likewise, many fine clubhouses remain without their original ethnic constituency.

Forming Alliances and Consortia.

Private clubs have found that collaboration fosters resource sharing and can leverage more support. Examples include joint marketing, coordinated programming, and sharing of fixed facilities costs.

TO READ MORE ABOUT THE HISTORY OF ETHNIC AND FRATERNAL ORGANIZATIONS:

Baldwin, Jen. "Top Five Irish Fraternal Orders you need to include in your family history search." Irish Central: Nov. 30, 2015. https://www.irishcentral.com/roots/top-five-irish-fraternal-orders-you-need-to-include-in-your-family-history. Accessed July 15, 2019.

Bodnar, John. St. Paul: Immigration History Research Center, University of Minnesota, 1981, 5–14. https://hsp.org/sites/default/files/legacy_files/migrated/bodnarbenassocreadingact1.pdf

Burke, Charles (former President of Charitable Irish Society of Boston). "The Silver Key: A History of the Charitable Irish Society, 1737-1973." https://www.charitableirishsociety.org/resources/Transfer%20History%20Folder/Silver%20Key%20Burke%20Binder%20FINAL.pdf.

Hays, Samuel P., editor. "City At The Point: Essays on the Social History of Pittsburgh." Pittsburgh: University of Pittsburgh, 1989.

Loomis, Bill. "Clubbing in Days Past: When Fraternal Societies Ruled". October 10, 2015. https://www.detroitnews.com/story/news/local/michigan-history/2015/10/10/fraternal-societies-detroit-history/73514852/

Metress, Seamus P. and Eileen K. Irish in Michigan. East Lansing: Michigan State University Press, 2006. Discovering the Peoples of Michigan series.

Meyer, B.H. "Fraternal Beneficiary Societies in the United States." P.646-661. Under the auspices of the Ethnical Subcommittee of the Committee of Fifty. 1902. Available through JSTOR.

Rose, Danielle. "Bohemian National Hall." Cleveland Historical. https://clevelandhistorical.org/items/show/739

Sarna, Jonathan D. (1978). "From Immigrants to Ethnics: Toward a New Theory of "Ethnicization." Ethnicity. 5.

Shashkevich, Alex. "Stanford scholar examines development of Mexican social clubs in Los Angeles." Stanford News, August 23, 2017. https://news.stanford.edu/2017/08/23/history-mexican-social-clubs-development-influence/ accessed July 22, 2019.